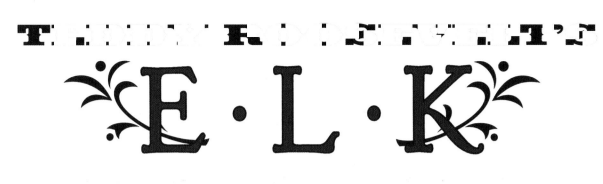

E·L·K

Brenda Z. Guiberson   **illustrated by Patrick O'Brien**

Henry Holt and Company   New York

To all the people who continue to
preserve the wild and unusual places
-B. Z. G.

To Allison, as always
-P. O'B.

Henry Holt and Company, Inc. *Publishers since 1866*, 115 West 18th Street, New York, New York 10011. Henry Holt is a registered trademark of Henry Holt and Company, Inc. Text copyright © 1997 by Brenda Z. Guiberson. Illustrations copyright © 1997 by Patrick O'Brien. All rights reserved. Published in Canada by Fitzhenry & Whiteside Ltd., 195 Allstate Parkway, Markham, Ontario L3R 4T8.

Library of Congress Cataloging-in-Publication Data
Guiberson, Brenda Z. Teddy Roosevelt's elk / Brenda Z. Guiberson; illustrated by Patrick O'Brien.
Summary: Follows a year in the life of a mother elk, her calf, and a bull in the Olympic Mountains of Washington State, where these animals are named in honor of President Roosevelt. 1. Roosevelt elk—Juvenile literature. 2. Roosevelt, Theodore, 1858-1919—Juvenile literature. [1. Roosevelt elk. 2. Elk. 3. Roosevelt, Theodore, 1858-1919.] I. O'Brien, Patrick, ill. II. Title. QL737.U55G85 1997 599.65'7—dc21 96-52144

ISBN 0-8050-4296-2 / First Edition—1997. Designed by Meredith Baldwin. The artist used oil paint on canvas to create the illustrations for this book. Printed in the United States of America on acid-free paper.∞
10 9 8 7 6 5 4 3 2 1

It is an early June morning, 1884, in the Dakota territory of the western United States. Teddy Roosevelt ties up his bedroll and then for breakfast dips two hard biscuits into a cup of hot coffee. As the sun warms the sky, he hikes up a steep hill and looks out to find elk and buffalo grazing as far as the eye can see.

Teddy Roosevelt watches all morning, writing in his journal about the bull with a broken antler, the call of a bobwhite, and the small elk calf that stumbles in a prairie-dog hole. He loves this wide open country, but is troubled by the rapid disappearance of its animals and trees. He closes his journal, but thoughts of the changing landscape stay with him.

As Teddy Roosevelt returns to camp, another elk calf is born. This calf is faraway from the plains, well hidden in the forests of the Olympic Mountains to the northwest. The calf rests quietly on soft moss near a salmonberry bush. Mother elk hurries to lick him clean so that black bears and wolves will not smell him. Soon the calf struggles up on long, tottering legs for his first drink of milk.

After two weeks, the spotted calf prances behind his mother
as they come up to a small herd of cows and calves. Mother
elk is the leader. The animals snort and grunt when she
returns. She shows her calf the best place to eat buttercups
and then scrapes bark from a tree with her teeth to mark this
territory. But the little calf trots up to a salmonberry bush
and nibbles the green leaves and pinkish red berries.

Mother elk wanders off to graze with other cows but one
cow stays behind to watch over the playful calves.

It is late afternoon. The herd is back together and mother elk leads them on a trail into the valley. Her calf jumps and slips down the hillside when a huge fly bites him on the nose. Mother elk nudges him back to a safe place in the middle of the herd. Soon the animals are drinking cold freshwater from a stream. Some of the cows wade deep into the water to get away from a swarm of biting blackflies.

High above them, on a windy slope, a great bull looks for food. He is eight years old and every year new antlers grow on his head like tree branches–thicker and longer than the year before. A fuzzy velvet skin protects the new bone. Already the antlers are two feet long and still growing almost an inch a day. *Chomp! Gulp!* The bull quickly swallows oat grass and tiny trees and takes no time to chew his food. He needs to eat constantly to keep his antlers and nine-hundred-pound body healthy and strong. Between bites he sniffs the air and twitches his ears as he checks for signs of danger.

Suddenly, he hears a snap! A gray wolf springs up behind him. Another comes out of the shadows and bares his teeth.

The bull kicks out with a sharp hoof and then bolts into the forest. He runs with his head back to keep the antlers from catching on low branches. After two quick miles, the wolves are no longer behind him. He stops in the shade of a cedar tree.

While the elk rests, he coughs the plants back up from his first stomach where food is stored. With long, slow chewing, he grinds all the tough stringy fibers into a soft mash. *Gulp!* Then he swallows the ground-up cud, which passes through his other three stomachs before it's finally digested.

After a rainstorm, mother elk and her calf walk into a meadow to eat mushrooms and ferns. The herd follows. As they graze, one cow after another looks up for signs of danger but only a marmot whistles from a rocky ledge. More dark clouds blow in from the ocean and rain begins again. The herd rushes under an umbrella of ancient trees, where huge branches keep them warm and dry.

On a hot day in August, the great bull scrapes the dangling velvet from his antlers. Now fully grown at four feet long and weighing a total of thirty pounds, the antlers no longer need their velvet for protection. The bull stomps and snorts as he rubs against the tree. Then his thrashing tears a salmonberry bush apart and the berries leave a red stain on his antlers. When he finally settles down under a tree, two small voles skitter up to eat the velvet tatters on the ground.

Now the great bull is ready to fight. In September he bellows across a foggy meadow and joins mother elk and the herd. Soon another bull arrives. The intruder bugles and wails and shakes his antlers. Both bulls want to claim this family group. They rear up on their hind legs and circle around, twisting their necks and snorting.

Suddenly, the great bull charges. *Rattle. Crunch.* The huge animals rear up and crash together again and again. The calf and his mother stop eating and watch the battle. *Whack!* The great bull twists quickly and bangs the side of the other elk with his antlers. The exhausted newcomer runs away. This time the great bull is stronger. But constant challenges from other bulls will leave him little time to eat or rest if he is to become the father of next year's calves.

In November the hair on the elk changes from reddish brown to light gray as it grows into a thick winter coat. The cows and calves stay together, but the great bull, tired and thin from his battles, goes off on his own.

One night a sudden storm covers the mountains with heavy snow. Mother elk leads the herd on a quick migration into the lowlands where the snow is not so deep. Soon the valley fills with other herds. It is a hard winter with little for them to eat. The calf paws the snow with his sharp hooves to nibble at the ryegrass beneath.

The great bull struggles through the frozen foothills. His antlers are a heavy burden to carry through the snow. He joins other bulls standing by an icy stream. They rear up on their hind legs to reach moss that dangles from the low branches. As the snow continues to fall, the smallest bull collapses and dies. He does not have enough fat needed to survive the winter.

The others find only a few rosehips and tough bushes to chew. Finally a strong wind swirls through the tops of the trees and blows down lichen and moss for the bulls to eat.

In mid-March, the great bull sheds his winter coat. Loose tufts of scruffy hair stick to the bushes as he chews on blackberry shoots and ferns. Soon his long antlers loosen and fall to the ground. Now he can walk under the lowest branches without hitting anything. But within a few days, new antlers begin to grow.

As the stream floods with melting snow, mother elk leads the herd on a slow migration back up the mountain. Her calf is beginning to grow small antlers, too. When they reach a shady cluster of trees, mother elk pushes him away. Like the other cows, it is time for her to find a quiet, hidden spot and have a new calf. The young elk wanders across the hillside to nibble green leaves and pink blossoms from a salmonberry bush. After a year in the mountains, he has learned to survive on his own.

Over that same year, Teddy Roosevelt has also learned about survival in the West. At a campsite hundreds of miles away, a cook yells loudly to wake everyone for the roundup. It is 3 A.M. and raining hard. Roosevelt eats a soggy breakfast before he saddles his horse and goes out to check on the cattle. When he rides into a gully after a stray cow, his horse can barely pass through the thick mud that slides down the treeless slopes. Bones of elk and buffalo lie scattered about. Roosevelt sees that hunters, loggers, and settlers have altered the landscape forever.

Soon Roosevelt will leave this rugged life and move back East to become a politician. He will work to preserve the American wilderness, ensuring a future in which the magnificent elk has a place to live.

Author's Note

In 1897 a scientist named C. Merriam Hart studied the elk in the Olympic Mountains in Washington State. These animals were bigger, had thicker antlers, and were darker colored than others he had seen. Hart named them Roosevelt Elk in honor of his friend Teddy Roosevelt.

Today Olympic National Park protects the largest population of Roosevelt Elk (five thousand animals) living in their natural habitat; although smaller numbers of these elk can also be found in areas of California, Oregon, Alaska, and British Columbia, Canada.

When Teddy Roosevelt was still a young man, elk herds roamed all across the United States. But extensive hunting caused the extinction of two elk subspecies and drastically reduced the populations of others. In 1909, as president of the United States, Teddy Roosevelt established Mount Olympus National Monument. Since then, thousands of new calves—just like the elk calf in this story—have grown up in these mountains. Wolves, however, have been heavily hunted and not been seen in this area for over fifty years.

During Teddy Roosevelt's presidency, fifty-one wildlife refuges, eighteen national monuments, five national parks, and almost 150 million acres of forests were preserved. As our great conservation president, he wrote, "We are not building this country of ours for a day. It is to last through the ages." Because of this legacy, these animals' lives are not very different from what they were one hundred years ago. The story of Teddy Roosevelt's elk is a testament to his vision and his gift to future generations.